ROYAL NAVY

INTERVIEW QUESTIONS

Sample interview questions and tips for the Royal Navy Officer
and Rating interviews

www.how2become.com

Orders: Please contact How2become Ltd, Suite 2, 50 Churchill Square Business Centre, Kings Hill, Kent ME19 4YU.

Please order via the email address: info@how2become.com.

ISBN: 9781909229624

First published 2013

Typeset for How2become Ltd by Molly Hill, Canada.

Printed in Great Britain for How2become Ltd by Bell & Bain Ltd, 303 Burnfield Road, Thornliebank, Glasgow G46 7UQ.

CONTENTS

GOING FOR OFFICER SELECTION?

ATTEND A 1-DAY ROYAL NAVY OFFICER
PREPARATION TRAINING COURSE.

Visit the following website to find out more:

www.NavyOfficerCourse.co.uk

INTRODUCTION

Welcome to your new guide – How to pass the Royal Navy interview. This guide has been designed to help you prepare for the Royal Navy Officer and the Royal Navy Rating interviews, including the Admiralty Interview Board. The guide contains lots of sample interview questions, answers and preparation advice that is suitable for both sets of selection.

The author of this guide, Richard McMunn, has over twenty years combined experience in the Royal Navy and the Emergency Services. He has vast experience and knowledge in the area of Armed Forces recruitment, and you will find his guidance both inspiring and highly informative. During his successful career in the Fire Service, Richard sat on many interview panels assessing candidates seeking to join the Service. He has also been extremely successful at passing job interviews and assessments himself, with a success rate of over 90%. Follow his advice and preparation techniques carefully and you too can achieve the same level of success in your career.

Whilst the selection process for joining the Royal Navy as either an Officer or as a Rating is highly competitive, there are a number of things you can do to improve your chances of success, and they are all contained within this guide.

The guide itself has been split up into useful sections to make it easier for you to prepare for each stage. Read each section carefully and take notes as you progress. Don't ever give up on your dream; if you really want to join the Royal Navy, either as an Officer or a Rating, then you can do it. The way to approach an application for a job in the Armed Forces is to embark on a programme of 'in-depth' preparation, and this guide will show you exactly how to do just that.

If you need any further help with the aptitude tests, planning exercises, getting fit or RN Officer Interview advice, then we offer a wide range of products to assist you. These are all available through our online shop www.how2become.com.

We are also now running a number of One Day Admiralty Interview Board preparation training courses at the following link:

www.NavyOfficerCourse.co.uk

Once again thank you for your custom, and we wish you every success in your ambition of joining the Royal Navy.

Work hard, stay focused and be what you want…

**Best wishes,
The How2become Team**

Disclaimer

Every effort has been made to ensure that the information contained within this guide is accurate at the time of publication. How2become Ltd is not responsible for anyone failing any part of the Royal Navy selection process as a result of the information contained within this guide. How2become Ltd and their authors cannot accept any responsibility for any errors or omissions within this guide, however caused. No responsibility for loss or damage occasioned by any person acting, or refraining from action, as a result of the material in this publication can be accepted by How2become Ltd.

The information within this guide does not represent the views of any third party service or HM Armed Forces.

CHAPTER 1

The Royal Navy Filter interview
and the new assessable competencies
(Suitable for both Officer and Ratings)

THE ROYAL NAVY FILTER INTERVIEW AND HOW TO PASS IT

During the Royal Navy selection process you will be required to sit interviews at both the Armed Forces Careers Office (AFCO) and, if applying to become an Officer, during your attendance at the Admiralty Interview Board (AIB).

Whilst the questions and tips contained within this section of the guide concentrate primarily on the AFCO interview, they are also great preparation for the AIB too. The interview, which is held at your local Armed Forces Careers Office, will be undertaken by a member of the Royal Navy recruitment team. The purpose of this interview is to 'filter' out those people who have the potential to join the Navy.

The duration of the initial AFCO interview will very much depend on your responses to the questions. However, you can expect the interview to last for approximately 30 minutes. The questions that you will be assessed against during the initial interview will normally be taken from the following areas:

- The reasons why you want to join the Royal Navy and why you have chosen this service over the Army or the Royal Air Force;

- Why you want to become a Royal Navy Officer, and what skills, qualities and experiences you have that would help you to become either a competent Officer or Rating;

- What choice of career you are most interested in, the reason for choosing that career, and the skills you have to match the role;

- What information you already have about the Royal Navy, its history, its lifestyle and training;

- Information relating to your hobbies and interests including sporting/team activities;

- Any personal responsibilities that you currently have at home, in your education or at work;

- Questions based around your ability to work as part of a team, leadership potential, confidence, resilience, planning, organising, communication skills, how you learn new skills or information and personal development;

- Information about your family and your partner and what they think about you joining;

- Information based around your initial application;

- Your experience of work and education;

- Your emotional stability and your maturity;
- Your drive and determination to succeed;
- Having a positive reaction to a disciplined environment and towards people in positions of authority.

Before I move on to a number of sample interview questions and tips for answering them, I want to explain a little bit about interview technique and how to come across in a positive manner during the interview. During my career in the Fire Service I sat on many interview panels assessing people who wanted to become fire-fighters. As you can imagine there were some good applicants and there were also some poor ones. Let me explain the difference between a good applicant and a poor one.

A good applicant

A good applicant is someone who has taken the time to prepare. They have researched both the organisation they are applying to join, and also the role that they are being interviewed for. They may not know every detail about the organisation and the role but it will be clear that they have made an effort to find out important facts and information. They will be well presented at the interview and they will be confident, but not over confident. As soon as they walk into the interview room they will be polite and courteous and they will sit down in the interview chair only when invited to do so. Throughout the interview they will sit upright in the chair and communicate in a positive manner. If they do not know the answer to a question they will say so and they won't try and waffle. At the end of the interview they will ask positive questions about the job or the organisation before shaking hands and leaving.

A poor applicant

A poor applicant could be any combination of the following. They will be late for the interview or even forget to turn up at all. They will have made little effort to dress smart and they will have carried out little or no preparation. When asked questions about the job or the organisation they will have little or no knowledge. Throughout the interview they will appear to be unenthusiastic about the whole process and will look as if they want the interview to be over as soon as possible. Whilst sat in the interview chair they will slouch and fidget. At the end of the interview they will try to ask clever questions that are intended to impress the panel.

Interview technique

How you present yourself during the interview is important. Whilst assessing candidates for interviews I will not only assess their responses to the interview questions, but I will also pay attention to the way they present themselves. A candidate could give excellent responses to the interview questions, but if they present themselves in a negative manner, this can lose them marks.

In the build-up to your initial AFCO interview practise a few 'mock' interviews. Look to improve your interview technique as well as working on your responses to the interview questions.

More recently, the Royal Navy updated its assessment criteria for the interview. In particular, it determined that the following areas will now be assessed:

- **Team working** - This could include examples of being a part of sports teams, group organisations and work. Ideally, competency examples should be within the last year.

- **Resilience** - You will be required to describe your physical fitness preparations including swimming. You need to demonstrate an understanding of the challenges of serving in the Naval Service and how you have managed pressure in the past.

- **Problem Solving** - This should be a fairly recent example of when you have had to solve a problem and provide details of how you resolved the issue and what the outcome was. Examples could be from any activity you are involved in, including work.

- **Planning and Organising** - A recent event or activity that you have organised or planned.

- **Learning and Developing** - You should have a good understanding of the Naval Service and the job you want to do, including the terms and conditions of service, training, roles, and why you are attracted to the Naval Service in general and to your job in particular. You could also be asked about how you enjoy learning things and what you have done recently to develop or improve yourself.

- **Discipline** - Looking at your interaction with people in authority and how you react to rules. What responsibilities do you have?

- **Communication skills** - These will be assessed throughout the interview.

If I were preparing for the Royal Navy interview right now I would take each of the above assessable areas individually, and prepare a detailed response setting out the extent to which I meet its requirements. Your response to each question that relates to the above competency areas must be 'specific' in nature. This means that you must provide an example in which you have already demonstrated the skills required for that area. Do not fall into the trap of providing a 'generic' response that details what you 'would do' if the situation arose.

Try to structure your responses in a logical and concise manner. The way to achieve this is to use the 'STAR' method of interview question response construction:

Situation

Start off your response to the interview question by explaining what the 'situation' was and who was involved.

Task

Once you have detailed the situation, explain what the 'task' was, or what needed to be done.

Action

Now explain what 'action' you took, and what action others took. Also explain why you took this particular course of action.

Result

Explain what the outcome was following your actions and those of others. Try to demonstrate in your response that the outcome was positive as a result of the action you took.

Finally, explain to the panel what you would do differently if the same situation were to arise again. It is good to be reflective at the end of your responses. This demonstrates a level of maturity and it will also show the panel that you are willing to learn from every experience.

During the next section of the guide I have specifically provided sample questions and answers that cover the above competency areas. The chapters thereafter will cover the more generic questions, and questions aimed at candidates preparing for the Admiralty Interview Board.

TEAM WORKING

It is very important that you are capable of working as part of a team when you join the Royal Navy. After all, their motto is THE TEAM WORKS! I will now provide you with a few relevant sample questions that I would encourage you to prepare for.

SAMPLE QUESTION – Tell me about a time when you have contributed to the effective working of a team?

How to structure your response:

- What was the size and purpose of the team?
- Who else was in the team?
- What was YOUR role in the team? (Explain your exact role.)
- What did you personally do to help make the team effective?
- What was the result?

Strong response

To make your response strong you need to provide specific details of where you have worked with others effectively, and more importantly where YOU have contributed to the team. Try to think of an example where there was a problem within a team and where you volunteered to make the team work more efficiently. It is better to say that you identified there was problem within the team rather than that you were asked to do something by your manager or supervisor. Make your response concise and logical.

Weak response

Those candidates who fail to provide a specific example will provide weak answers. Do not fall into the trap of saying 'what you would do' if this type of situation arose.

Sample response

"I like to keep fit and healthy and as part of this aim I play football for a local Sunday team. We had worked very hard to get to the cup final and we were faced with playing a very good opposition team who had recently won the league title. The team consisted of eleven players who regularly spend time together during training sessions and at social events. After only ten minutes of play, one of our players was sent off and we conceded a penalty as a result. Being one goal down and 80 minutes left to play we were faced with a mountain to climb. However, we all remembered our training and worked very hard in order to prevent any more goals being scored. Due to playing with ten players, I had to switch positions and play as a defender, something that I am not used to. Apart from being a defender I felt my role was to encourage the other players to keep going and to not give up until the final whistle had sounded. All the other players supported each other tremendously and

the support of the crowd really pushed us on. The team worked brilliantly to hold off any further opposing goals and after 60 minutes we managed to get an equaliser. The game went to penalties in the end and we managed to win the cup. I believe I am an excellent team player and can always be relied upon to work as an effective team member at all times. I understand that being an effective team member is very important if the Royal Navy is to continually perform to a very high standard. However, above all of this, effective teamwork is essential in order to maintain the high safety standards that are set."

SAMPLE QUESTION - Do you have any experience of working as a team member?

The ability to work effectively in a team is an extremely important aspect of the role of Naval personnel. Not only will you be spending a great deal of time together at work, you will also depend on your colleagues during highly dangerous and stressful incidents. Therefore it is important that you can demonstrate you have the ability to work as an effective team member.

When responding to this type of question, try to think of occasions when you have been part of a team and achieved a common goal.

Maybe you are already involved in team sports playing hockey, rugby or football? You may also find that you have experience of working as a team member through work. If you have no or very little experience of working as a team member then try to get some before you apply to the Navy. After all, teamwork is an important aspect of the job.

Now take a look at the following sample response.

"Yes, I have many years' experience of working in a team environment.

To begin with, I have been playing hockey for my local team for the last three years. We worked really hard together improving our skills over the course of last season and we managed to win the league. I am also very much involved in teamwork in my current job. I work as a nurse at the local hospital and in order for the ward to function correctly we must work effectively as a team. My job is to check all of the patients at the beginning of my shift and also make sure that we have enough medical supplies to last the duration. It is then my responsibility to inform the ward sister that the checks have been carried out. She will then obtain more supplies if we need them. We have to work very closely together for many hours and we all pull together whenever the going gets tough. I enjoy working in a team environment and feel comfortable whilst working under pressure."

SAMPLE QUESTION - Do you enjoy working in a team environment?

The best answer for this type of question is to state that you very much enjoy working in a team environment and that you are adaptable and can work in any role within a team. When answering this type of question try to give examples of situations where you have been an effective team member and achieved a common goal. The following sample response is better geared towards someone who has worked in an office environment prior to applying for the Royal Navy.

"In a previous role I was required to work as part of a 30-strong sales team. I really enjoyed the atmosphere within that team and managed to learn so much from other members. Yes I do enjoy working in a team environment but conversely my adaptability allows me to work in any environment. I would say that I can work either as one of a team or an individual depending on the requirements of the role. If I am required to work as part of a team then I will always listen carefully to the provided brief by my officer-in-command, keep in communication with the other team members, support those people who need supporting in the team, and also learn from any mistakes that the team makes so that we can improve next time.

I can remember one particular occasion when I was required to work as part of a team. Sales figures for the month were low and we were required to work as a team in order to generate new business leads. We all came together as a team and discussed the different options available to us. My role within the team was to source potential new clients over a two-week period whilst others sent out promotional materials once I had created the new leads. As a team we managed to increase sales and revenue by 50% in just a short space of time."

SAMPLE QUESTION - Give an example of when you have had to work as a team.

During your response to this question you MUST provide a specific situation where you have previously worked as a team. Take a look at the following sample response which will give you some good pointers for constructing your own.

"I have had lots of experience to date working as part of a team. In my current role as a bricklayer I have been working on a project with many other skilled workers and labourers. The project involves building ten new houses within a three-month period. We are now half way through the project and it is running smoothly and on time.

During this particular project I have been required to work with people who I did not know before the start of the build. This has not been a problem for me as I have no issue with working with anyone, regardless of who they are. I always start off by introducing myself to the rest of the team and ask the other team members to introduce themselves. This acts as a bit of an ice-breaker and it gets everyone talking.

At the start of each working day we listen carefully to the brief provided by the fore-man. As we work through the tasks set by the foreman we communicate with each other clearly so that everyone knows what is going on and whereabouts we all are with the project. If anyone in the building team starts to slow up we all gather round to help them catch up. As a team member I am always focused on the end goal and work very hard to carry out my job meticulously and diligently."

SAMPLE QUESTION - What would you do if a member of your team was not pulling their weight or doing their job effectively?

This question would be more appropriate for someone applying for Officer Entry.

Take a look at the following sample response to this question.

"I would first of all ask them if there was anything wrong, or if there was anything I could do to support them. The member of the team might be having personal is-sues, and if this was the case, I would want to support them and help them through it. If it was simply a case of them being lazy, then I would take immediate action to stop it. I would take them to one side and tactfully point out to them how important their role was within the team. I would inform them that without their full attention on the task in hand we would not be able to achieve our goal. I would also consider discipline procedures if appropriate and/or remedial training."

RESILIENCE

When preparing your responses to questions based on resilience I recommend you provide details about your physical fitness activity (including swimming) and also a demonstration of how capable you are at handling the pressures of serving in the Royal Navy. I have now provided a couple of questions to help you prepare.

SAMPLE QUESTION – What have you done to prepare for life in the Royal Navy and tell me a bit about your fitness activity?

"I have been preparing for the selection process for a number of months now. To begin with I have been finding out about life within the Navy and the types of challenges I will have to face, such as taking responsibility for myself and my actions and also coping with being away from home for long periods of time. To assist me in my preparation for life within the Navy I have taken on lots of extra duties and responsibilities at home and around the house. For example, every day I clean one area of the house thoroughly and I am also responsible for ironing everyone's clothes in the household. This has been great practise for my training course, if I am to be successful.

With regards to my fitness I have been working very hard in this area. Although I am already a competent swimmer I have been going to my local pool four times a week and each time I swim 50 lengths of the 25 metre pool using a variety of different strokes. I have also been getting up at 6 a.m. each morning and running three miles each time, just to get used to the early starts.

I fully understand that life will be tough when I start the training course, but I am fully prepare for what lies ahead and I believe I have the maturity and responsibility to make sure I am successful and above all an asset to the Royal Navy team."

SAMPLE QUESTION - Provide an example of where you have completed a task despite pressure from others. What did you do and what did you say?

"In my current job as car mechanic for a well-known company I was presented with a difficult and pressurised situation. A member of the team had made a mistake and had fitted a number of wrong components to a car. The car in question was due to be picked up at 2 p.m. and the customer had stated how important it was that his car was ready on time because he had an important meeting to attend. We only had two hours in which to resolve the issue and I volunteered to be the one who would carry out the work on the car. The problem was that we had three other customers in the workshop waiting for their cars too, so I was the only person who could be spared at that particular time. In order to solve the problem I first of all gathered

appropriate information. This included exactly what needed to be done and in what priority. I also established what realistically could be done and what couldn't be done in the time-frame given. I worked solidly for the next two hours making sure that I meticulously carried out each task in line with our operating procedures. Even though I didn't finish the car until 2.10pm, I managed to achieve all of the tasks under pressurised conditions whilst keeping strictly to procedures and regulations."

SAMPLE QUESTION – Provide an example of where you have had to make a difficult decision despite pressure from other people.

"My son is in his final year at the local school. To date, his work has been exceptional and every parents evening we attend he is praised by his teachers. However, recently there was an incident that involved very poor judgment on my son's part. He got involved with a group of youths from school who were bullying a boy who was less fortunate than themselves. The matter was brought to my attention by the boy's Father. He contacted me by letter and explained that my son had allegedly been involved in the bullying behaviour with the other youths. I immediately asked my son if the allegations were true. He immediately owned up to his part in the bullying, much to our disappointment. I decided that the best course of action was to take my son into school and to make the Head Teacher aware of the situation with a view to my son being punished in line with the school's disciplinary procedures. My wife totally disagreed with my planned course of action and started to put pressure on me to deal with this within the family environment.

However, I maintained my stance. I was determined that my son should be punished by the school first and foremost. By taking this course of action I believed that my son would learn from his mistake and that he would never carry out this dreadful act again. I also wanted to ensure that the other offending youths were punished by the school too, as this would act as a deterrent to anyone else in the school who was thinking of bullying an individual.

Whilst my wife still disagreed with me to this day I believe the course of action I took was appropriate given the seriousness of the situation. My son was punished by the school and has since maintained a very high level of discipline both at school and at home."

SAMPLE QUESTION - How do you keep yourself fit and why do you think fitness is important to the role of someone serving in the Royal Navy?

"Yes, I keep myself fit and active and it is an important part of my life. I go swimming three times a week and swim 30 lengths every time I go. I go jogging twice a week to break up the routine and mix in some light weight work at the gym every now and again.

I also play football for my local Sunday team, which involves one practise session every fortnight. Plus I ensure that I eat a proper diet, which helps to keep me feeling confident and healthy.

Yes, I think that fitness is vital to the role of someone serving in the Royal Navy. The role involves working long hours and coupled with the fact that the work can be physically demanding, it is important that Royal Navy Officers and Ratings stay fit and healthy so that they can perform to their peak and cope with the demands of the job."

PLANNING AND ORGANISING

Being able to plan and organise is all part and parcel of Royal Navy life. Make sure you can provide examples of when you have planned or organised an event. You should also be able to provide examples of how you keep your life organised and also provide details of what you do in your spare time. Make sure you use your spare time wisely and constructively!

SAMPLE QUESTION - Provide an example of where you have taken personal responsibility to arrange or organise an event or situation?

"After reading an appeal in my local paper from a local charity, I decided to try to raise money for this worthwhile cause by organising a charity car wash day at the local school during the summer holidays. I decided that the event would take place in a month's time, which would give me enough time to organise such an event.

I set about organising the event and soon realised that I had made a mistake in trying to arrange everything on my own, so I arranged for two of my work colleagues to assist me. Once they had agreed to help I asked one of them to organise the booking of the school and arrange local sponsorship in the form of buckets, sponges and car wash soap to use on the day, so that we did not have to use our own personal money to buy them. I asked the second person to arrange advertising in the local newspaper and radio stations so that we could let the local community know about our charity car wash event, which would in turn hopefully bring in more money on the day for the charity.

Following a successful advertising campaign, I was inundated with calls from local newspapers about our event, and it was becoming hard work having to keep talking to them and explaining what the event was all about. But I knew that this information was important if we were to raise our target of £500.

Everything was going well right up to the morning of the event, when I realised we had not got the key to open the school gates. It was the summer holidays so the caretaker was not there to open the gates for us.

Not wanting to let everyone down, I jumped in my car and made my way down to the caretaker's house and managed to wake him up and get the key just in time before the car wash event was due to start. In the end the day was a great success and we all managed to raise £600 for the local charity."

SAMPLE QUESTION – Tell me what you get up to in your spare time or at weekends?

"I like to use my time wisely and I don't like sitting around doing nothing. More recently my time has been spent preparing for the selection process. Therefore, I have been getting up every day at 6 a.m. and going for a run before work. During lunchtime I have been reading my literature about the Royal Navy and studying for this interview too. When I get home in the evenings I sometimes go swimming and then I will often go and play five-a-side football with my friends.

When it comes to the weekends I still keep fit and active by going on long and challenging walks, or going camping with friends. I am very much an active person who likes to make the most of the outdoors."

PROBLEM SOLVING

Taking personal responsibility to solve problems yourself is very much part of life within the Royal Navy, which is why you will probably be asked to provide an example of when you have solved a problem on your own or as part of a team.

SAMPLE QUESTION - Provide an example of where you have solved a difficult problem. What did you do?

"I was working in a retail shop and it was a busy trading day in the run up to Christmas. We had been advertising a promotion for a new brand of perfume in the local press that was due to launch the very next day. All of a sudden a member of staff approached me and informed me that no stock of the new perfume had been delivered and that time had run out to get any delivered before the following day's trade commenced. This obviously spelt disaster for the company as many people had placed pre-orders of the new perfume and they would be coming in to the store to collect their goods.

I started off by calling a meeting of three key members of staff. We gathered in the staff room and I coordinated a brain storming session in order to resolve the issue. I started off by gathering as much information as possible. The key facts I gained were:

1. The amount of time we had left in order to get some stock delivered.
2. How much stock we needed to fulfil pre-orders.
3. Who was available to work late that evening?
4. Who had transport and a full driving licence?

Once I had gathered the facts I then developed a plan to resolve the problem. I asked a member of the team to phone around all company stores in the county to establish which shops had extra stock. I then assigned another member of staff who was willing to work late to drive out to the stores in order to borrow the extra surplus stock. I then personally placed an initial order with the distributer so that we had enough stock to fulfil orders for the entire Christmas period and to also pay back the stock we had borrowed from other stores in the County.

The result of the situation was that we managed to obtain sufficient stock to fulfil the orders the next day. Finally, I carried out a full investigation as to why this situation had occurred in the first place with a view to making sure it never happened again."

SAMPLE QUESTION - Provide an example of where you have solved a problem in a work situation?

"I was working at a restaurant and noticed a divide between the waiters and kitchen staff. This was a problem that had to be resolved as it was impacting on the effectiveness of the team. Most of the kitchen staff were older than their waiter colleagues and had migrated from India. There was very little interaction between the kitchen and waiter staff colleagues and I was concerned that this barrier would not only make the kitchen staff feel isolated, but that it would also have a negative impact on the team environment.

My initial considerations were to ensure that the kitchen staff felt comfortable and that they could speak to me and the waiters if they needed help or assistance. After all, they had not been in the country for long and I wanted them to feel welcome and valued. I believe that communication between colleagues within a workplace is essential to achieve the best possible results and create a good working environment, regardless of individual differences.

To overcome the challenges I introduced myself to all the kitchen staff members and I learnt their names. This ensured that they felt valued, and that they also had a point of contact if they ever needed assistance or support. I also encouraged the other waiters to communicate with their kitchen colleagues. Following my actions communication improved and the workplace is now a more efficient and happier working environment."

LEARNING AND DEVELOPING

Continuous development during your career in the Royal Navy is very important. Therefore, during the interview you will probably be asked to provide details of an occasion on which you have learnt a new skill, or improved an existing one.

SAMPLE QUESTION - Tell me about a time when you have taken it upon yourself to learn a new skill or develop an existing one?

How to structure your response:
- What skill did you learn or develop?
- What prompted this development?
- When did this learning or development occur or take place?
- How did you go about learning or developing this skill?
- What was the result?
- How has this skill helped you since then?

"Although I am in my late twenties I had always wanted to learn to play the guitar. It is something that I have wanted to do for many years, but have never had the time to learn until recently. One day I was watching a band play with my wife at my local pub and decided there and then that I would make it my mission to learn to play competently. The following day I went onto the Internet and searched for a good guitar tutor in my local area. Luckily, I managed to find one within my town who had a very good reputation for teaching. I immediately booked a block of lessons and started my first one within a week. My development in the use of playing the guitar progressed rapidly and I soon achieved grade one standard. Every night of the week I would dedicate at least 30 minutes of time to my learning, in addition to my one hour weekly lesson. I soon found that I was progressing through the grades quickly, which was due to my level of learning commitment and a desire to become competent in playing the instrument.

I recently achieved grade four and I am now working to grade five standard. I am also now playing in a local band, and the opportunities for me, both musically and socially, have increased tenfold since learning to play. In addition to this, learning to play the guitar has improved my concentration levels and my patience."

SAMPLE QUESTION - Tell me about a time when you changed how you did something in response to feedback from someone else?

'During my last appraisal, my line manager identified that I needed to improve in a specific area. I work as a call handler for a large independent communications company. Part of my role involves answering a specific number of calls per hour. If I

do not reach my target then this does not allow the company to meet its standards. I found that I was falling behind on the number of calls answered and this was identified during the appraisal. I needed to develop my skills in the manner in which I handled the call. My line manager played back a number of recorded calls that I had dealt with and it was apparent that I was taking too long speaking to the customer about issues that were irrelevant to the call itself. Because I am a conscientious and caring person I found myself asking the customer how they were and what kind of day they were having. I was spending too much time on delivering a high quality service to the customer, as opposed to working through the call as fast as possible so that I could answer the next one.

Despite the customers being more than pleased with level of customer care, this approach was not helping the company and therefore I needed to change my approach. I immediately took on-board the comments of my line manager and also took up the offer of development and call handling training. After the training, which took two weeks to complete, I was meeting my targets with ease. This in turn helped the company to reach its call handling targets.'

DISCIPLINE

You don't need me to tell you how important discipline is in a career such as the Royal Navy, but how you answer the questions based around this competency is very important. You need to be able to demonstrate that you can take instructions from people in senior positions, and also demonstrate how self-disciplined you are either at home, in education or in a work setting. Before you attend the Royal Navy interview be able to provide answers to questions like these. Here is a sample question and answer to help you prepare.

SAMPLE QUESTION – can you give an example when you have followed instructions or guidelines in order to complete a task?

"Whilst working in my current role as a gas engineer I was tasked with fitting a new boiler to a domestic property. I carried out this work unsupervised and was relied upon to follow strict procedural and safety guidelines. If I did not follow the procedural guidance that I received during my training then I would be putting lives at risk. I must ensure that I carry out my work responsibly and follow all safety procedures to ensure that my work is carried out in accordance with my company's policies. The boiler was fitted to the required standard in accordance with the relevant British Standard and all safety procedures were followed. The customer was satisfied with my work and I was happy that I carried out my duties responsibly. I fully understand the importance of being self-disciplined in the Royal Navy, and if you do not follow rules and procedures or follow instructions then this can endanger people's lives and also jeopardise a mission."

SAMPLE QUESTION - Tell me about your educational exam results. Were you satisfied with them and what did you think of your teachers and your school?

Many people leave school without the grades that they want. I was one of them! However, it's my opinion that what you do following your exam results is the most important thing. Despite only achieving three GCSE's at grade C or above I went on to achieve many qualifications after my initial school education was over. Apart from many Fire Service qualifications I more recently achieved a Diploma in Management, and various health and safety qualifications. The point I am trying to make here is that you can still achieve many things in life despite poor educational qualifications.

This question is designed to see what you personally think about your results, and also your attitude to your education and to people (your teachers) who are in positions of authority. If you didn't get the results that you wanted then just say so. However, it is important to tell the interviewer what you plan to do about them and what your plans are for the future. When I passed Armed Forces selection many years ago I had a six month wait before I could start my basic training. The Warrant Officer at the AFCO advised that I embarked on an educational foundation course at college for the six month period whilst I waited to commence my basic training. I took his advice and I am glad that I did.

Whilst responding to this interview question be positive about the future and tell the interviewer what you are currently doing to improve your academic skills. If you are applying to become an Officer then you will obviously have already met the minimum qualification requirements for the role; however, you should consider whether or not you could have achieved improved scores if you had applied yourself more effectively during your educational years.

The second part of the question is very important. Questions of this nature are designed to see how you react to discipline. Many of us probably did not get on with at least one of our teachers during our educational years; however, keep your personal opinions of your teachers to yourself and focus on displaying your ability to respect and understand the need for discipline.

SAMPLE QUESTION - Tell me about your educational exam results. Were you satisfied with them and what did you think of your teachers and your school?

'I did okay on the majority of exams but I wasn't satisfied with my Math's result. I know I could have done better. However, since my results I've working hard to improve my skills in this area and I have embarked on an evening course which will hopefully gain me a better grade. I am a determined person and I'm always looking to improve my skills. One of my strengths is that I can see what I need to work on and I always make sure I work hard to make the necessary improvements. In relation to my teachers and my school I have a lot of respect for them. The teachers are in positions of authority and it is important to respect that. I also understand that if I am successful in my pursuit to join the Royal Navy it will be very important to be disciplined at all times. Discipline is at the core of all operations and without it things can go wrong and tasks and objectives may not be met. I can be relied upon to maintain discipline at all times during my Naval career."

COMMUNUCATION SKILLS

How to improve your scores through effective communication

During the interview the interviewer will be looking to see how you communicate, and also how you structure your responses to the interview questions. Consider the following points both during the interview and whilst responding to the interview questions:

- When you walk into the interview room stand up straight and introduce yourself. Be polite and courteous at all times and try to come across in a pleasant manner. The panel will be assessing you as soon as you walk through the door so make sure you make a positive first impression.

- Do not sit down in the interview chair until you are invited to do so. This is good manners.

- When you sit down in the interview chair, sit up straight and do not fidget or slouch. It is acceptable to use hand gestures when explaining your responses to the questions but don't overdo it, as they can become a distraction.

- Structure your responses to the questions in a logical manner – this is very important. When responding to an interview question, start at the beginning and work your way through in a concise manner, and at a pace that is easy for the panel to listen to.

- Speak clearly and in a tone that is easy for the panel to hear. Be confident in your responses.

- When talking to the panel use eye contact but be careful not to look at them in an intimidating manner.

- Wear a formal outfit to the interview such as a suit. You are applying to join the Armed Forces, which is a disciplined environment. Therefore, you need to demonstrate that you are capable of dressing smartly and also taking pride in your appearance.

Final golden interview tips

- Always provide 'specific' examples to the questions being asked that are based around competencies.

- During your responses try to outline your contributions and also provide evidence of the competency area that is being assessed.

- Speak clearly, use correct English and structure your responses in a logical and concise manner.

Now let's take a look at a number of generic sample interview questions. Please note that these questions are not guaranteed to be the exact ones you'll come up against at the real interview, but they are good starting point in your preparation. Use the sample responses that I have provided as a basis for your own preparation. Construct your answers on your own opinions and experiences. Once again, it does not matter whether you are applying for Rating entry or Officer, you should still prepare for every question contained within the section.

CHAPTER 2

Generic questions for the Royal Navy
interview (Suitable for both
Officer and Ratings)

Sample interview question number 1

Why do you want to join the Royal Navy?

This is an almost guaranteed question during the initial interview so there should be no reason why you can't answer it in a positive manner. Only you will know the real reason why you want to join but consider the following benefits before you construct your response:

- A career in the Royal Navy is challenging. You will face challenges that are not usually faced in normal jobs outside of the Armed Forces. These challenges will make you a better person and they will develop you into a professional and competent member of a proud organisation;

- A career in the Royal Navy will not only give you the chance to develop your skills and potential but it will also give you excellent qualifications and training;

- A career in the Royal Navy will give you the chance to travel and see different cultures. This alone will broaden your horizons and make you a more rounded person;

- The Royal Navy, like the other Armed Forces, is an organisation that people have a huge amount of respect for. Therefore those people who join it are very proud to be a part of such a team.

Try to display a good level of motivation when answering questions of this nature. The Royal Navy is looking for people who want to become a professional member of their team and who understand their way of life. It should be your own decision to join and you should be attracted to what this career has to offer. If you have been pushed into joining by your family then you shouldn't be there.

Sample response to interview question number 1

Why do you want to join the Royal Navy?

'I have been working towards my goal of joining the Royal Navy for a number of years now. A couple of years ago a careers advisor visited our school to talk about the Royal Navy. After his presentation I went up to him and asked a few questions about the different career options that were available. In particular I was most interested in the role of an Officer as I believe I have the leadership and management potential to succeed in this role. Since that day I have set my sights on joining this organisation and I have been working hard to improve myself. To be honest, I want a career that will give me direction, professional training, qualifications and the chance to work with people who set themselves very high standards. I have spoken to a friend who already works in the Royal Navy as a pilot and he fully recommends it.

I've looked at the different career options outside of the Royal Navy and nothing matches up to the challenge or the sense of pride I would feel by joining a team like this. I am the captain of the school rugby squad and being part of a winning team is something that I very much enjoy. Even though I am quite capable of working on my own I much prefer to work in a team where everyone is working towards the same goal. Finally, even though I have a good stable home life I can't wait to leave home and see what's out there. Even though travelling isn't the be-all and end-all, I am looking forward to visiting different countries and experiencing varied cultures. Many of my friends have never been out of their home town but that's not for me. I want to broaden my skills and get some decent training in the process and I believe that I would be a great asset to the Royal Navy.'

Sample interview question number 2

Why have you chosen the Royal Navy over the Army or the Royal Air Force?

As you know, there are three main forces that you can apply to join. The Royal Navy is different to the other forces in the way that you'll be required to serve on board ship for many months of your career. To some, this is not appealing. Personally I enjoyed my time on board ship. I spent my time in the Fleet Air Arm which meant that I didn't spend half as much time on board ship as the other branches of the Royal Navy. Other branches will live on board ship 365 days a year, even when it is dockside. You need to be fully comfortable with this fact and be 100% certain that you can cope with the demands of living on board. Personally I believe there is nothing better than being on board ship and when you do arrive back home after a long trip it makes you appreciate your home soil even more.

The Royal Navy will give you ample variety and it will also give you many different career options. As an Officer or Rating you will receive the highest standard of training available. The Officers with whom I served were excellent leaders, motivators and a real inspiration to the team. Conversely, the Ratings I worked alongside were excellent team workers, extremely hardworking and great comrades. The amount of activity, skills and experience that I crammed into my Royal Navy career was unbelievable. You won't get that in any other job!

Take a look at the following sample response to this question before creating your own based on your own views and opinions.

Sample response to interview question number 2

Why have you chosen the Royal Navy over the Army or the Royal Air Force?

'I did consider the other forces and even had a chat with each of the careers advisors but at the end I was still set on the Royal Navy. I even sat down with my parents

and we wrote down the benefits of each of the different services and the Royal Navy came out on top in all aspects. I have always had a keen passion to work on aircraft and it is my intention to become an Aircraft Engineer. The Fleet Air Arm is my first choice because I would get to work on board ship in addition to working on aircraft. During my research I visited the Fleet Air Arm museum at HMS Heron and I was fascinated by the history and the aircraft that have formed part of the service over the years.

I have thought long and hard about my choice of career and I am fully aware of the training that I will undergo if I am successful. I've been working hard to pass the selection process and I am 100% certain that the Royal Navy is for me. If I am un-successful at this attempt then I will look at what I need to improve and work hard for next time.'

Sample interview question number 3

What does your family think of you wanting to join the Royal Navy?

What your family think about you wanting to join the Royal Navy is very important, simply for the reason that you will need their support both during your training and during your career. I can remember my parents being fully behind my decision to join the Royal Navy and I'm glad that they were for a very good reason. After about two weeks into my basic training I started to feel a little bit home sick; like any young man would do being away from home for a long period of time. I rang my father and discussed with him how I felt. After about five minutes chatting on the phone I felt perfectly fine and I no longer felt homesick. During that conversation he reminded me how hard I had worked to get a place on the course and that he and my mother wanted me to succeed. For that reason alone I was glad that I had the support of my parents.

Before you apply to join the Royal Navy it is important that you discuss your choice of career with either your parents or your guardian. If you have a partner then obviously you will need to discuss this with them, too. If they have any concerns whatsoever then I would advise you take them along with you to the Armed Forces Careers Office so they can discuss these concerns with the trained recruitment staff. Get their full support as you may need it at some point during your career, just like I did.

There now follows a sample response to help you prepare.

Sample response to interview question number 3

What does your family think of you wanting to join the Royal Navy?

'Before I made my application I discussed my choice of career with both my parents and my girlfriend. Initially they were apprehensive but they could see how motivated

and excited I was as I explained everything I had learnt so far about the service. I showed them the recruitment literature and we even planned a trip to the Fleet Air Arm museum so they could see what I would be joining. I understand that it is important they support me during my application and I now have their full backing. In fact, they are now more excited about the fact I'll be leaving home than I am! I have also told them everything I know about the training I will go through and the conditions I will serve under. They are aware that the Royal Navy has a brilliant reputation and this has helped them to further understand why I want to join.

Sample interview question number 4

What grades did you achieve at school and how do you feel about them?

Questions that relate to your education and more importantly what you thought of your results are common during both Officer and Rating interviews. In addition to this question they may also ask you questions that relate to which schools or educational establishments you attended.

This kind of question is designed to assess your attitude to your grades and also how hard you worked whilst at school, college or university. As you can imagine, your grades will generally reflect how hard you worked and therefore you will need to be totally honest in your response. Naturally you must meet the minimum eligibility requirements for joining the Royal Navy before you can apply, but how well you did at school or university academically might also be a reflection as to how well you will do during initial and on-going training. If your results were not as good as you anticipated then you will need to provide a good reason for this. If you achieved the grades you wanted during education then congratulations, you'll find this question easier to answer.

Take a look at the following sample response, which is tailored towards a person who did not do as well as they wished.

Sample response interview question number 4

What grades did you achieve at school and how do you feel about them?

'To be totally honest I didn't do as well as I had hoped. The reason for this was that I didn't work hard enough during the build-up to the exams. I did put in some preparation but I now realise I should have worked harder. Whilst I passed the exams I know that I could have done a lot better. I fully appreciate that I will have several exams and assessments to pass during initial training and I have been preparing for this. I have embarked on an evening class at my local college to maintain my competence in Maths and English and I am constantly studying Naval facts and history. My current affairs knowledge is excellent and I have been enjoying the study time

immensely. I can assure you that, even though I should have done better at university, I have learnt from this and I am working very hard to prepare for initial training in the anticipation that I am successful at the selection interview.

Sample interview question number 5

What responsibilities do you have either at work, school or at home?

When you join the Royal Navy as an Officer you will need to take full responsibility for yourself, your team, your equipment and also for the safety of your work colleagues. As a Rating you will also need to take responsibility for yourself and the safety of your equipment and work colleagues. At the age of eighteen I was responsible for servicing and maintaining Sea Harrier jets on board HMS Invincible. I was responsible for going out on deck at 4 a.m. and servicing the ejector seats that formed part of the pilot's safety equipment. That was a huge responsibility to undertake at such a young age. Whatever branch you decide to join you will need to demonstrate during selection that you can handle responsibility. The most effective way to do this is by providing the interviewer with examples of where you have already held positions of responsibility either at home, work or during your education.

Take a look at the following sample response to this question.

Sample response to interview question number 5

What responsibilities do you have either at work, school or at home?

'I currently hold a large number of responsibilities both at home and in my part-time job. I am responsible for cleaning the house top to bottom once a week and I usually do this on a Sunday before I go and play football for my local team. I'm also captain of the football team which means I have to arrange the fixtures, book the football ground and I also collect the kit at the end of the match and get it washed and dried for the following week's fixture. I also take control of the clubs financial affairs as I have an interest in accountancy. I thoroughly enjoy this responsibility and would not have it any other way; I am always the first to volunteer for any task or role that involves a level of responsibility. In addition to this I have just started a new part-time job at my local supermarket as a junior supervisor. This involves managing five members of staff, managing stock levels and also managing resources. It is essential that I make sure the store has sufficient resources to operate effectively every day that it is open.

I enjoy taking on responsibility as it gives me a sense of achievement. I understand that I will need to be responsible during my Royal Navy training not only for myself, but also for ensuring that I work hard to pass every assessment in order to develop into a competent member of the Royal Navy establishment.

Sample interview question number 6

How do you think you will cope with the discipline, regimentation and routine in the Royal Navy?

When you join the Royal Navy you will be joining a military organisation that has set procedures, standards and discipline codes. Procedures, standards and discipline codes are there for a very good reason. They ensure that the organisation operates at its optimum level. Without them things would go wrong, and people would either be injured or possibly killed. As an Officer you will have the added responsibility of ensuring those underneath your command respect these important codes of conduct and policies. To some people these important aspects of service life will come as a shock when they join. The recruitment staff will want to know that you are fully prepared for this change in lifestyle, regardless of whether you are joining as a Rating or an Officer. The Royal Navy is investing time, effort and resources in your training so they want to know that you can cope with their way of life.

When answering this type of question you need to demonstrate both your awareness of what Royal Navy life involves and also your positive attitude towards the disciplined environment. Study the recruitment literature and visit the careers website to get a feel for the type of training you will be going through.

Sample response to interview question number 6

How do you think you will cope with the discipline, regimentation and routine in the Royal Navy?

'I believe I would cope with it very well. In the build up to selection I have been trying to implement routine and discipline into my daily life. I've been getting up at 6 a.m. every weekday morning and going on a three mile run. This will hopefully prepare me for the early starts that I'll encounter during training. I've also been learning how to iron my own clothes and I've been helping around the house with the cleaning and washing. I already have to follow and manage codes of conduct in my part-time job. Being responsible for five members of staff I am required to monitor their performance, brief them on new policies and procedures, and also carry out annual appraisals.

I fully understand that the Royal Navy needs a disciplined workforce if it is to function as effectively as it does. Without that discipline things could go wrong and if I did not carry out my duties professionally then I could endanger somebody's life.

NOTE: If applying for Officer Entry you should consider adding this to your response:

"I am also aware that I will be required to manage discipline within my team once

I am a qualified Officer. I am fully prepared for this and would carry out my duties diligently, professionally and competently."

Sample interview question number 7

How do you think you will cope with being away from home and losing your personal freedom?

This type of question is one that needs to be answered positively. The most effective way to respond to it is to provide the recruitment staff with examples of where you have already lived away from home for a period of time. This could be either with your school or college, an adventure trip, camping with friends or even with a youth organisation. Try to think of occasions when you have had to fend for yourself or even 'rough it' during camps or adventure trips. If you are already an active person who spends very little time sat at home in front of the television or computer, then you will probably have no problem with losing your personal freedom. During your time in the Navy there'll be very little time to sit around doing nothing anyway. So, if you're used to being active before you join, then this is a plus.

Take a look at the sample response on the following page and try to structure your own response around this.

Sample response to interview question number 7

How do you think you will cope with being away from home and losing your personal freedom?

'I already have some experience of being away from home so I know that this would not be a problem for me. Whilst serving with the Sea Cadets I was introduced to the Navy way of life and I fully understand what it is like to be away from home. Having said that, I am not complacent and I have been working hard to improve my fitness and academic skills. To be honest with you, I'm not the kind of person who sits around at home watching television or sitting at the computer, so I'm hardly indoors anyway. In terms of losing my personal freedom I'm looking forward to the routine and regimentation that the Navy will provide as I believe this will bring some positive structure to my life. Even though I am young I want to ensure that I have a good future and I believe a career in the Royal Navy will bring me just that, providing that is, I work hard during training.

During my time in the Sea Cadets I've been away on a couple of camps and I really enjoyed this. We learnt how to fend for ourselves whilst away and I loved the fact that I was meeting new and interesting people. I understand that the training will be difficult and intense but I am fully prepared for this. I am confident that I will cope with the change in lifestyle very well.'

Sample interview question number 8

Are you involved in any sporting activities and how do you keep yourself fit?

During the selection interview you will be asked questions that relate to your sporting activities and also how you keep yourself fit.

If you are the type of person who spends too much time on the computer or social networking sites then now's the time to make a positive change. Even though you'll be on board ship there will still be time for sporting activities. Whilst on board HMS Invincible I really got into my weight training. Right at the bottom of the ship there was a small gym, and even though it was usually packed full of Royal Marines, there was still time to keep fit. On the odd occasion when the flight deck wasn't being used for flying operations it was opened up for running and general sports such as volleyball. All of these helped to keep up the team morale on board ship.

Sample response to interview question number 8

Are you involved in any sporting activities and how do you keep yourself fit?

'I am an extremely fit and active person and I am currently involved in a couple of sports teams. To begin with, I visit the gym four times a week and carry out a light weight session before swimming half a mile in the pool. Sometimes I like to vary the gym session with a workout on the indoor rowing machine. In the build up to selection I have been getting up at 6 a.m. every weekday morning and going on a three mile run. This I believe will prepare me for the early starts during selection.

I am also a member of my local hockey team and I practise with them one evening a week during the season. We usually play one match a week which forms part of a Sunday league table. We are currently third in the table and are pushing hard for the top spot. Finally, I am a keen hill walker and love to take off for long walks in the Lake District or Brecon Beacons with some of my friends. We usually camp out for a couple of nights over a weekend so I am used to fending for myself. I am not the type of person who just sits at home on the computer or playing video games. I love being active and always keep myself fit.'

Sample interview question number 9

What do you think the qualities of a good team player are?

Remember the Royal Navy motto? 'The team works'. I have already made reference to the importance of teamwork during this guide and there is a possibility that you will be asked a question that relates to your ability to work as part of a team and also what you think the qualities of an effective team worker are. Whilst on board ship there is a high risk that things can go wrong. You are hundreds of miles away from land and any support from other ships could be hours away. If something serious goes wrong then you have to work very fast and professionally as part of a team in order to resolve the issue. Before you can work effectively as a team however you need to know what the main qualities of a competent team member include. Take a look at the following:

- An ability to interact and work with others, regardless of their age, sex, religion, sexual orientation, background, disability or appearance;
- Being able to communicate with everyone in the team and provide the appropriate level of support and encouragement;
- Being capable of carrying out tasks correctly, professionally and in accordance with guidelines and regulations;
- Being focused on the team's goal(s);
- Having a flexible attitude and approach to the task;
- Putting the needs of the team first before your own;
- Putting personal differences aside for the sake of the team;
- Being able to listen to others' suggestions and contributions;

When responding to this type of question it would be an advantage if you could back up your response with an example in which you already work in a team. Take a look at the following sample response before creating your own based on your own experiences and ideas.

Sample response to interview question number 9

What do you think the qualities of a good team player are? (Officer applicant)

'A good team player must have many different qualities including an ability to listen carefully to a given brief. If you don't listen to the brief that is provided then you can't complete the task properly. In addition to listening carefully to the brief you must be able to communicate effectively with everyone in the team. As a Royal Navy Officer this will be even more important. As a team member and leader I will be responsible for supporting the other team members and also listening to other people's suggestions about how a task can be achieved. You also have to be able to work with anyone in the team regardless of their age, background, religion, sexual orientation, disability or appearance. You can't discriminate against anyone and if you do, then there is no place for you within that team. A good team player must also be able to carry out his or her job professionally and competently. When I say competently I mean correctly and in accordance with guidelines and training. You should also be focused on the team's goal and not be distracted by any external factors. Putting the needs of the team first is paramount. Finally a good team player must be flexible and be able to adapt to the changing requirements of the team.

I already have some experience of working in a team and I know how important it is to work hard at achieving the task. I have a job working in my local supermarket as a junior supervisor and every week we have a team briefing. During the team briefings it is my responsibility to inform the team what tasks need to be carried out as a priority. During one particular meeting I asked the team to clear a fire escape that had become blocked with cardboard boxes, debris and rubbish. In addition to this I also asked the team to come up with a plan to prevent it from happening again. Once I had briefed the team members we all set about the task carefully removing the rubbish. Once this was completed we then worked together in order to devise a plan to prevent it from happening again. Whilst it is important to delegate work as a leader, it is just as important to be able to work as part of that team, encouraging, supporting and communicating as you progress through the task.

Sample interview question number 10

What do you do in your spare time?

Questions of this nature are designed to assess how effectively you use your spare time. If you are an inactive person who sits in watching television most days then you are less likely to adapt to the change in lifestyle the Navy will bring than if you are a fit, active and sporty type of person. Take a look at the following two lists which differentiate between positive ways to spend your spare time and negative ways.

Positive ways to spend your spare time

- Brisk walking, running, gym work, swimming, cycling, indoor rowing;
- Studying for exams or academic qualifications;
- Preparing for a goal or aspiration such as joining the Royal Navy;
- Team activities such as football, hockey, rugby etc;
- Outdoor activities such as mountaineering, orienteering, mountain biking or climbing;
- Charity or voluntary work.

Negative ways to spend your spare time

- Sitting at home watching television or playing computer games;
- Spending hours on social networking sites;
- Sitting on park benches or being on the streets doing nothing;

Now take a look at the following sample response to this question which will assist you in your preparation.

Sample response to interview question number 10

What do you do in your spare time?

'During my spare time I like to keep active, both physically and mentally. I enjoy visiting the gym three times a week and I have a structured workout that I try and vary every few months to keep my interest up. When I attend the gym I like to work out using light weights and I also enjoy using the indoor rower. I always try to beat my best time over a 2000 metre distance.

I'm also currently doing a weekly evening class in Judo, which is one of my hobbies. I haven't achieved any grades yet but I am taking my first one in a few weeks. I'm also a member of the local Sea Cadets, which is an evening's commitment every week and the occasional weekend. Of course, I know when it is time to relax and usually do this by either listening to music or playing snooker with my friends but, overall, I'm quite an active person. I certainly don't like sitting around doing nothing. I understand that if I'm successful in joining the Navy then there will be lots to keep me occupied in the evenings, especially during my basic training.'

Sample interview question number 11

Can you tell me about any achievements you have attained during your life so far?

Those people who can demonstrate a history of achievement during the Royal Navy interview are far more likely to pass the initial training course. Therefore, demonstrating a history of achievement already will work in your favour. Having achieved something in your life demonstrates that you have the ability to see things through to the end, something which is crucial to your career in the Navy as a Rating or as an Officer. It also shows that you are motivated and determined to succeed.

Try to think of examples where you have succeeded or achieved something relevant in your life. Some good examples of achievements are as follows:

- Winning a trophy with a football or hockey team;
- GCSE's, 'A' Levels, Degrees and other educational qualifications;
- Duke of Edinburgh's Awards;
- Being given responsibility at work or at school;
- Raising money for charity.
- Keeping physically fit and playing team sports.

Sample response to interview question number 11

Can you tell me about any achievements you have experienced during your life so far?

'Yes I can. So far in my life I have achieved quite a few things that I am proud of. To begin with I achieved good grades whilst at school in both my GCSE's and 'A' levels. I worked very hard to achieve my grades and I'm proud of them. At weekends I play rugby for a local team and I've achieved a number of things with them. Apart from winning the league last year we also held a charity match against the local Police rugby team. We managed to raise £500 for a local charity which was great achievement.

More recently I managed to achieve a huge increase in my fitness levels in preparation of the Pre-Joining Fitness Test. Before I started my preparation I couldn't reach the minimum standard required but I have since worked very hard and I can now easily pass the required target for my age group.

Sample interview question number 12

What are your strengths and what are you good at?

This is a common interview question that is relatively easy to answer. The problem with it is that many people use the same response. It is quite an easy thing to tell the interviewer that you are dedicated and the right person for the job. However, it is a different thing backing it up with evidence!

If you are asked this type of question make sure you are positive during your response and show that you actually mean what you are saying. Then, back up the strengths you have mentioned with specific examples which demonstrate the quality you are claiming to possess. For example, if you tell the panel that you are a motivated person, back it up with an example in your life where you have achieved something through sheer motivation and determination.

Sample response to interview question number 12

What are your strengths and what are you good at? (Officer Applicant)

'To begin with, I'm a determined person who likes to see things through to the end. For example, I recently ran a marathon for charity. I'd never done this kind of thing before and found it very hard work, but I made sure I completed the task. Another strength of mine is that I'm always looking for ways to improve myself. As an example, I have been preparing for the Navy Officer selection process by embarking

on an evening class that will see me eventually achieve a Diploma in Management Studies. Although I have a small amount of managerial and supervisory experience, I want to make sure that I am in the best position possible for becoming a competent Royal Navy Officer. Finally, I would say that one of my biggest strengths is that I'm a great team player. I really enjoy working in a team environment and achieving things through a collaborative approach. For example, I play in a local rugby team and we recently won the league trophy for the first time since the club was established some 50 years ago.'

Sample interview question number 13

What are your weaknesses?

Now this is a difficult question to answer! We all have weaknesses and anyone who says they haven't, is probably not telling truth. However, you must be very careful how you respond to this question. Apart from being truthful you must also provide a weakness that you are working hard on to improve. You should also remember that you are joining a disciplined service that requires hard work, determination and a will to succeed. So, if you are the type of person who cannot get up in the morning and you keep making regular mistakes at work or at school, then the Royal Navy might not be for you.

The key to responding to this type of question is to be truthful but to also back it up with examples of what you are doing to improve your weakness. Take a look at the following example.

Sample response to interview question number 13

What are your weaknesses?

'My biggest is weakness is that sometimes I work too hard. Once I get in from my day job I am straight upstairs working on my computer, studying for a course I have undertaken. Whilst being hard working is a positive aspect of my character, I do need to learn to relax and take time out. I will never be a lazy person and I really do get a lot out of working, but I must take more time to relax as this will help me to perform better when I am at work."

Sample interview question number 14

Why do you want to become an Officer? Why don't you become a Rating instead? (Officer Applicant)

This type of question is designed to see if there are any genuine reasons why you have chosen to become an Officer. Some applicants get carried away with the perceived glamour and status of the role, without putting any serious thought into why they actually want to become an Officer. When preparing your response to this question you need to think about the skills and attributes that you have already gained that are relevant to the role of a Royal Navy Officer. You may already have some genuine reasons why you want to become an Officer but please read the following sample response which will give you some good pointers when preparing your response.

Sample response to interview question number 14

Why do you want to become an Officer? Why don't you become a Rating instead? (Officer Applicant)

'I have thought long and hard about applying to become a Officer and I am fully certain that this is what I want to do. To begin with, I spent considerable time assessing my own qualities and attributes and I believe they would be most suited to that of an Officer. I am hard working, tenacious, resolute, professional, driven and ambitious and feel that these qualities will allow me to eventually become a competent Officer in the Royal Navy. In addition to my qualities I have already gained some experience in a supervisory role within my current job. I really enjoy the additional responsibility that this brings and would not thrive in a role that holds little or no responsibility. It is my ultimate goal to join the Royal Navy and serve as an Officer. I am determined and resolute and believe that I would make an invaluable contribution to this elite service.'

Sample interview question number 15

What are the different ranks for both Royal Navy Officers and Ratings?

This question assesses your knowledge of the ranks within the Royal Navy. It is a simple question and one that should be relatively easy to respond to. Having an understanding of the different ranks for both commissioned and non-commissioned staff will be an obvious advantage for when you start your initial training. Here are the ranks within the Royal Navy for you to study:

Admiral of the Fleet

Admiral

Vice-Admiral

Rear Admiral

Commodore

Captain

Commander

Lieutenant-Commander

Lieutenant

Sub-lieutenant

Midshipman

Warrant Officer 1

Warrant Officer 2

Chief Petty Officer

Petty Officer

Leading Rate

Rating

RATINGS

OFFICERS

You may also decide to study the different markings for each rank prior to your interview. These can be viewed at the Royal Navy's website www.royalnavy.mod.uk.

Further sample interview questions

Q16. Tell me about the basic training you will undergo as an Officer? (NOTE: If you are applying for Officer Entry it is advisable that you have knowledge of the Rating's selection training too; after all, if you are managing Ratings as an Officer then you should have knowledge of the type of training they will undergo!

Q17. Tell me about the basic training you will undergo as a Rating?

Q17. What is the minimum service contract you will be required to sign as an Officer or a Rating?

Q18. Which part of your training do you think you would find the hardest?

Q19. What have you been doing so far to prepare for the Admiralty Interview Board? (Officer Applicants)

Q20. If you fail Officer selection, would you consider joining as a Rating?

FINAL INTERVIEW TIPS

Within this section of the guide I will provide you with some final tips that will help you prepare for the filter interview. Remember that your success will very much depend on how *prepared* you are. Don't forget to work on your interview technique, carry out plenty of research and work on your responses to the interview questions.

- In the build-up to the interview carry out plenty of targeted preparation work. Read your recruitment literature and spend time studying the Royal Navy website. Ask the AFCO recruitment advisor to provide you with further information about the training you'll undergo. If you get the opportunity, speak to serving members of the Royal Navy to find out as much as possible about life within the Service.

- Work on your interview technique and make sure you try out at least one 'mock interview'. This involves getting your family or friends to sit you down and ask you the interview questions that are contained within this guide;

- When you receive your date for the interview make sure you turn up on time. Check your travel and parking arrangements the day before your interview. The last thing you need is to be late for your interview!

- Think carefully about what you are going to wear during the interview. I am not saying that you should go out and buy an expensive suit but I do recommend you make every effort to dress smartly and formally. Having said that, if you do decide to wear a smart suit or formal outfit, make sure it is clean and pressed. You can still look scruffy in a suit.

• Personal hygiene is all part and parcel of Royal Navy life. Don't attend the interview unwashed, dirty or fresh from the building site!

• When you walk into the interview room, stand up straight with your shoulders back. Project an image of confidence and be polite, courteous and respectful to the interviewer at all times;

• Don't sit down in the interview chair until invited to do so. This will display good manners;

• Whilst you are in the interview chair sit upright with your hands resting on your knees, palms facing downwards. It is acceptable to use your hands expressively, but don't overdo it;

• Don't slouch in the chair. At the end of each question readjust your position;

• Whilst responding to the interview questions make sure you speak up and be positive. You will need to demonstrate a level of motivation and enthusiasm during the interview;

• Go the extra mile and learn a little bit about the Royal Navy's history. When the panel asks you **"What can you tell us about the Royal Navy?"** you will be able to demonstrate that you have made an effort to look into their history as well as their modern day activities;

• Ask positive questions at the end of the interview. Don't ask questions such as "How much leave will I get?" or "How often do I get paid?"

• If you are unsure about a question do not to 'waffle'. If you do not know the answer, then it is acceptable to say so. Move on to the next question and put it behind you. Remember, you are being assessed against your communication skills, so a bit of preparation in this area will not go a miss!

• Finally, believe in yourself and be confident.

CHAPTER 3

The AIB scoring criteria
(OFFICER APPLICANTS)

THE AIB SCORING CRITERIA

Before I go on to explain the scoring criteria, let us first of all take a look at some of the competencies required to successfully pass the Royal Navy Officer initial training course at Britannia Royal Naval College (BRNC). Having an understanding of these will help you prepare better for the interview.

Competencies Required for Success during Initial Officer Training

INTERPERSONAL COMPETENCIES

Communicating effectively	Is able to communicate accurately and effectively both orally and in writing.
Teamwork	Is able to work with others to achieve common goals.
Influencing	Can influence others to follow a certain course of action.

INTERPERSONAL COMPETENCIES

Appreciation	Comprehends, identifies, extracts and assimilates information from a range of sources, quickly and accurately.
Reasoning	Thinks logically, practically and coherently to produce a successful or reasonable solution, quickly and accurately.
Organisation	Determines priorities and allocates resources effectively and efficiently to a task(s).
Capacity	Holds and processes multiple inputs whilst maintaining task performance.

CHARACTER COMPETENCIES

Decisiveness	Makes sound appropriate decisions within time-scale demanded by the situation.
Self-motivation	Demonstrates a high level of commitment and interest to tasks.
Self-analysis	Monitors and objectively analyses own performance.

Integrity	Behaviour is guided by principles, morals and ethics appropriate to service life. Adheres to rules and regulations specific to the Royal Navy.

Now that we understand some of the competencies that are required to pass Royal Navy Initial Officer Training, we can explore the type of qualities the assessors will be looking for during the Admiralty Interview Board.

EXAMPLES OF COMPETENCIES ASSESSED DURING THE ADMIRALTY INTERVIEW BOARD

EXAMPLE COMPETENCY	DESCRIPTION
Communication	• Delivers communication in a concise and effective manner, both written and orally. • Listens to others' suggestions. • Contributes when appropriate. • Understands the situation/discussion.
Teamwork	• Is able to work with others in order to achieve a task or goal. • Puts in plenty of effort. • Treats others appropriately. • Supports other team members. • Communicates with the team. • Encourages the team.
Influencing	• Has considerable impact on others. • Can persuade and direct others.
Problem Solving	• Can judge certain situations. • Is flexible. • Is decisive. • Can come up with solutions to most problems.
Confidence and Resilience	• Self-assured. • Is composed and calm. • Acts with a sense of urgency when required. • Can be assertive is required. • Perseveres. • Determined. • Resolute.

When are the competencies assessed?

Each of the qualities will be assessed during every stage of the AIB, although some more than others. For example, you will be assessed on your influencing capabilities considerably during the planning exercise and your teamwork skills during the Practical Leadership Task (PLT) when you are not in command. You can begin to understand now why it is not important to find out what tasks you are going to undertake during the AIB. What is important is that you perform and behave in accordance with the Personal Qualities and the Core Competencies being assessed. For the interviews which form part of the AIB, you should concentrate on demonstrating ability and competence in every single area!

CHAPTER 4

How to pass the Admiralty
Interview Board Interview

HOW TO PASS THE ADMIRALTY INTERVIEW BOARD INTERVIEW

During this section of the guide I will provide you with a number of sample interview questions and advice on how to answer them. This section is only appropriate for candidates who are attending the Admiralty Interview Board. Whilst some of the questions will appear to be easy to answer, it is still important that we cover them, in order to ensure that you are fully prepared for you AIB. You will find that some of the questions in this section are duplicated. The reason for this is simply because some people who use this book will only be interested in the AIB section.

I have divided the sample questions into various different sections to assist you during your preparation.

Section 1 - Personal questions

Questions that are based on your personal details are obviously very easy to answer. However, you need to ensure that your responses demonstrate you have the key skills and attributes to carry out the role of an Officer. After some of the questions I will provide tips on how I believe you should answer them.

Q. Where are you living now and who are you living with?

Whilst it is acceptable for you to still live with your parents, the assessor may be looking for a level of independence here. If you do live with your parents then state that this has been a temporary measure whilst you prepare for Royal Navy selection. Tell the interviewer that you are fully independent at home and that you have lots of responsibilities, such as ironing, cleaning and also some financial responsibilities too.

Q. Where else have you lived apart from with your parents?

Again, aim to demonstrate a level of independence. If you have lived with other people during your early life then it may be easier for you to adapt to life in training, on-board ship and whilst serving in the Royal Navy in general.

Q. Describe your home life to me?

I am certainly not telling you what to say here; however, if it was me answering this question I would be looking to tell the interviewer that my home life was stable yet disciplined. I would also inform

them that I had plenty of responsibilities whilst at home, including cleaning, ironing and also financial responsibilities. Having said that, it is absolutely fine to tell the panel if your home life was unsettled – what is important is what you have learnt from your experiences and how they have helped you to prepare for RN life as an Officer.

Q. What was your life like growing up?

Questions that relate to your home life are designed to assess how stable you are as person, whether or not you have any responsibilities at home, whether you are generally a happy person and also what you have learnt from life's experiences to date.

Things to consider:

- Know key dates of where you have lived.
- Try and provide examples of where you have moved around. This demonstrates that you are flexible and adaptable when the need arises.
- It is preferable that your home life is stable.
- The more responsibilities you have at home, such as washing, ironing, cleaning, financial responsibilities etc, the better.
- If you have lived with other people, apart from your immediate family, tell them so. Remember – as a Royal Navy Officer you will be living with men and women of different ages etc.

Education

Q. How many schools have you attended and what years did you attend them?

Q. What did you think about your teachers?

Do not, under any circumstances, be disrespectful about your teachers when answering this question – if you do, the chances of passing AIB will be slim! Remember that you are applying to join a disciplined service and therefore, it is crucial that you demonstrate respect for people in positions of authority, regardless of whether you liked them or not!

Q. Tell me about your exam results; did you achieve the grades you wanted?

Q. Could you have worked harder whilst at school?

Although these are relatively easy questions to respond to, ones that relate to your exam results and how hard you worked whilst at school could catch you out. You have to be honest about your results. If they were not up to the standard that you expected, have a valid reason why. Never be disrespectful of your teachers or the educational system. Remember that you are applying to join a disciplined service.

School/college

Q. Did you learn anything from other students?

During the first section of this interview guide I provided you with sample responses to questions based around 'learning and developing'. This question gauges whether or not you have the ability to learn from others. Regardless of who we are or how old we are, we can ALL learn from others. My advice would be to think of a situation you have been in where you have learnt from other people, either in an educational-based scenario or work-based one.

Q. Did you have any responsibilities whilst at school or college?

If you are applying to become an Officer then it is important you demonstrate previous experience of having assumed responsibility or leadership of a project or other people. Good examples to use here would be if you were the captain of a football or hockey team, or even Head of Year!

Q. What sports did you participate in whilst at school or college?

If you didn't participate in any sports at school then you need to have a good reason why not! Being active and playing team sports is not only great for your physical and mental fitness, but it is also essential for your leadership and team working capabilities. When talking at interview about the sports you are or have been involved in, talk with a level of enthusiasm and also talk about any trophies or competitions you won. Being an 'achiever' is something the panel will want to see here as it will demonstrate to them that you have the ability to complete tasks to a high standard.

Q. What clubs or societies were you a member of?

Q. Do you have the Duke of Edinburgh or similar awards?

Being a member of a team or society is a positive thing, simply because being in the Royal Navy is very much like being part of a winning team! Try and give positive examples of teams, clubs or organisations you have been a part of during your life.

Q. Where did you travel to with school?

Previous experience of travelling with other people is good, simply because that's what you will be doing when you join the Royal Navy.

Q. Did you have any gaps in your education?

If you did have any gaps in your education, it is better to say that you used the time wisely. Maybe you went travelling around the world in order to gain new experiences and cultures, or maybe you wanted to take time out from your studies to take on a work related role or even a charity role. Whatever you do, do not say that you did nothing with your time off. If you went travelling, what did you gain from the experience?

Whilst at school or college it would be an advantage if you had some level of responsibility. For example, maybe you were a prefect or head of year, or maybe you were the captain of a sports team. You are applying to become an Officer, which effectively means you are going to be a manager and a leader. Having some previous experience of these important roles will be an advantage. If you haven't had any responsibilities in your life to date, how do you know that you'll be a good leader or manager in the Royal Navy?

Outside interests and hobbies

When responding to questions based on your interests and hobbies I recommend that you provide ones that demonstrate you are both active and a team player. Interests that also demonstrate your ability to learn new skills are also positive attributes to mention.

Q. What sports are you currently engaged in?

Try and provide sports that involve teamwork, such as:
- *Rugby;*
- *Hockey;*
- *Football;*
- *Netball.*

I also advise that you become a competent swimmer prior to applying to join the Royal Navy, if you are not already.

Q. What sporting achievements have you gained?

If you can provide any proof of sporting achievements, either as part of a team or individually, then great! The panel will want to see evidence of achievements you have gained to date, as this will provide reassurance that you are more likely to complete the tough recruitment course. Demonstrating a history of achievement is very important when applying to join the Royal Navy.

Q. Have you been part of any youth organisations such as the Scouts, Guides, Sea Cadets?

Q. Describe your hobbies and interests?

Positive things to mention here include:
- *Team sports*
- *Individual sports*
- *Walking and mountaineering*
- *Cycling*
- *Swimming*
- *Yoga or Pilates*
- *Camping and orienteering*
- *Playing a musical instrument*

Q. Are you currently employed either full-time or part-time?

If you are already employed then this is a positive thing to tell the interview panel. If you are not employed, either full-time or part-time, then you will need to provide reasons why you have not taken on any form of employment. If you are still in education then there is no reason why you cannot find part-time work. If it is simply a case that you have not been able to find any form of employment then you might wish to consider finding a voluntary role to carry out as this will give you invaluable experience of working with others.

Q. What did you used to do during your school holidays?

A great response to this interview question is to say that you were always active during the school holidays and playing team sports. You love the outdoors and would often go camping with your friends or go off on expeditions. If you enjoy travelling then this is a good thing to tell the interview panel as it will demonstrate that you are comfortable with being away from home in different environments.

Q. Have you ever travelled? If so, where and when did you go and what did you gain from the experience(s)?

Q. What are your future ambitions or plans?

Here's how I would personally answer this question:

"My current ambition is to secure a job as an Officer with the Royal Navy. I then want to excel during the training course, learn as much as possible about the role and organisation and also be accepted by my peers. With regard to future ambitions, I would very much like to spend many years in the Royal Navy and progress through the ranks. However, it would be important for me to become competent and proficient in each role before I considered applying for promotion and to also have the backing and recommendation of my Senior Commanding Officer. In brief, I see my future and ambitions centred on a career in the Royal Navy."

Employment

If you have no experience in a work related role to date, how do you know that you will be a good employee for the Royal Navy? Make sure you have some work experience under your belt, even if it's part time work or charity work. Try to also provide examples of responsibilities during each work role, and any managerial experience too. These will all work in your favour.

Q. What responsibilities have you had during any jobs you have undertaken to date?

Q. Why did you leave each job?

It is far better to say that you left a job to find a new challenge than you left because the pay was poor or the job was uninspiring! Here's a good response to this question:

"I decided to leave this particular job because I felt I had learnt all that I could within the role. I thoroughly enjoyed my time with the employer but it was time for me to leave and seek a new and more demanding challenge."

Q. Did you complete any courses or gain any qualifications during each job?

Q. Who did you have to communicate with in each job?

Q. Were you part of a team or did you work alone?

Q. What were your appraisals like?

TIP

If your appraisals were good then this is a great thing to tell the panel. However, most people usually have an area of improvement identified during an appraisal. If this relates to you, make sure you tell the panel that you always take on-board the feedback provided by your line manager, and also that you implemented an 'action plan' for improvement immediately following your appraisal. Remember that one of the key attributes for joining the Royal Navy is the ability to 'learn and develop'.

Motivational questions

Q. Why do you want to join the Navy? Have you considered the RAF or the Army?

Q. What specifically attracts you to the Royal Navy?

Q. When did you first want to join and has anyone influenced you in your decision to join?

TIP

Nobody should have influenced you to join – the decision should be your own following extensive research into the role and the organisation.

Q. Who have you talked to about a career in the Royal Navy?

Q. How many visits have you had to the Armed Forces Careers Office?

TIP

It is better to say that you had five visits than just the one! This will show how keen and enthusiastic you are about joining and absorbing all there is to know about the Royal Navy.

Q. Have you previously attended AIB? If you have, what have you done to improve on last time?

If you have been to AIB before and failed, it is imperative that you provide details about how you have worked on your weak areas. If you attend the AIB for a second time without having improved, there is very little chance of you passing. For example, if you failed the first time due to your fitness levels (or lack of them), provide comprehensive details of the work you have been doing in order to improve.

Q. What contact have you had with the Royal Navy? Have you visited any establishments or spoken to any serving members?

Visiting Royal Navy establishments prior to going to AIB is a positive thing. There are many different establishments you could attend, including museums!

Q. Are there any disadvantages for you joining?

There should be no disadvantages to you joining the Royal Navy.

Q. What do your family and friends think of you joining?

Q. What branch of the Royal Navy have you applied for?

Q. Would you consider any other branches of the Navy other than the one(s) you have chosen?

Here's how I would personally answer this interview question:

"I have been working very hard toward my selected branch and I have my heart set on joining it. Having said that, my priority lies with joining the Royal Navy and if the selectors deem I would be more suited to another branch then I would certainly consider it. Having said that, I do very much want to join my chosen branch and I hope that with continued hard-work and dedication this will become a reality."

Q. What research have you carried out during your preparation for joining the Royal Navy?

You obviously need to demonstrate that you have carried out lots of research about the Royal Navy, the different branches, your training and current operations.

Q. Would you consider a Non-Commissioned role if you were unsuccessful at AIB?

Here's how I would personally answer this question:

"My aim is to become an Officer with the Royal Navy and therefore I would not want to join as a Rating. If I was unsuccessful at this attempt then I would want to go away and work hard on my identified weak areas. I strongly believe I have the right qualities, attributes and determination levels to become a competent Officer and I won't give up until I prove to the assessors that I have the potential to become part of their team."

Q. What length of commission/service would you like to work?

Q. What qualities are required in order to become a Royal Naval Officer?

Defend your branch choice as much as possible. In order to be capable of achieving this, you will need to know it inside out. Make sure you research key information about your chosen branch/career.

Knowledge of the Royal Navy

Q. Tell me what you know about the history of the Royal Navy?

Q. What training will you undergo as an Officer?

Q. Do you think you will have any problems or face any challenges during Initial Officer Training?

Q. Have you learnt anything about other branches of the Royal Navy? For example, if you are applying to join the Fleet Air Arm, what do you know about the Engineering section?

Q. Tell me what you know about the different aircraft that serve in the Royal Navy?

Q. Tell me what you know about the different ships that serve in the Royal Navy?

Q. Tell me what you know about the different types of weapons that are carried both on ships and on our aircraft?

Q. How would you feel about going to war?

Q. Where are the UK bases of the Royal Navy?

Q. Whereabouts in the world is the Royal Navy operating right now?

Current affairs questions

Current affairs are a very important area of your preparation. You must carry out plenty of research in relation to current affairs. Not only will you need it during the interview(s), but it will also assist you during the essay element of the AIB.

Here are a few important tips to help you research current affairs effectively:

Tip 1 – Be careful what paper(s) you read. The type of paper you read will reflect you as a person. If you tell the interviewer that you are an avid reader of the Sun or the Daily Star, you may not be officer material. In the build up to AIB, try reading the Times, or another quality newspaper.

Tip 2 – I would strongly recommend that you subscribe to 'The Week'. This is a fantastic journal that will break down the week's stories for you. It will save having to buy lots of different newspapers.

You can subscribe to the week at the following website:

www.theweek.co.uk

Tip 3 – Consider reading the Economist. Once again, this is a quality journal that will provide you with lots of current affairs information.

You can subscribe to the Economist at the following website:

www.economist.com

Tip 4 – Don't just research affairs that are relevant to the Royal Navy or the Armed Forces in general. Other topics are just as important!

The purpose of the current affairs section of the AIB interview is designed to assess how informed you are about current global affairs. You should have a general view on each subject and have an understanding of why the issue is important. Try to have a general view of the whole world with knowledge of a number of issues and events.

Use this format to help you research news and current affairs events:

- What is the subject?
- Why is it significant?
- What is your opinion on it?

Sample current affairs questions

Q. Take me on a tour of the world and tell me what's caught your eye in the news recently.

Q. Tell me about six current affairs from abroad and six from home.

Q. Tell me about a news story from each continent.

USEFUL WEBSITES

BBC News – www.bbc.co.uk/news/

The Times Online – www.timesonline.co.uk

NATO (North Atlantic Treaty Organisation) – www.nato.int

Ministry of Defence – www.mod.uk

Army – www.army.mod.uk

Royal Navy – www.royalnavy.mod.uk

Royal Air Force – www.raf.mod.uk

FINAL INTERVIEW TIPS

- Research key affairs from across the world.
- Have a broad knowledge of current affairs.
- Research affairs that have happened in the last twelve months.
- Focus in detail on events in the last six months.
- Select six topics for 'home' affairs (e.g. the budget, gang culture).
- Select six topics for 'away' affairs. Make sure that you use examples from right across the world.
- Gauge an opinion of each affair (you will need to be able to argue your point).
- Know key facts: people, numbers, locations etc.
- A firm handshake demonstrates a lot about your character.
- Be to the point and concise (don't waffle).
- Hold even eye contact with each boarding officer.
- Avoid hesitations such as "erm, ah, umm etc".
- Don't use slang.
- Sit up straight and don't slouch.
- Be confident but not overly so!
- Learn the dates and events listed on your application form.
- Make yourself stand out - do something different.
- Be aware of your weaknesses.
- Identify your strengths.
- Think before you speak.

A FEW FINAL WORDS

You have now reached the end of the guide and no doubt you will be ready to start preparing for the Royal Navy Officer selection process. Just before you go off and start on your preparation, consider the following.

The majority of candidates who pass the selection process have a number of factors in common. These are as follows:

1. They believe in themselves.

The first factor is self-belief. Regardless of what anyone tells you, you can pass the AIB and you can achieve high scores. Just like any job of this nature, you have to be prepared to work hard in order to be successful. The biggest piece of advice I can give you is to concentrate on matching the assessable qualities that form part of the scoring criteria. These would be at the forefront of my mind if I were going through selection right now. Make sure you have the self-belief to pass the selection process and fill your mind with positive thoughts.

2. They prepare fully.

The second factor is preparation. Those people who achieve in life prepare fully for every eventuality and that is what you must do when you apply to become an Officer with the Royal Navy. Work very hard and especially concentrate on your weak areas. Within this guide I have spoken a lot about preparation. Identify the areas that you are weak on and go all out to improve them.

3. They persevere.

Perseverance is a fantastic word. Everybody comes across obstacles or setbacks in their life, but it is what you do about those setbacks that is important. If you fail at something, ask yourself 'why' have I failed? This will allow you to improve for next time and if you keep improving and trying, success will eventually follow. Apply this same method of thinking when you apply to join the Navy as an Officer.

4. They are self-motivated.

How much do you want to join the Royal Navy? Do you want it, or do you really want it? When you apply to join you should want it more than anything in the world. Your levels of self-motivation will shine through when you walk into the AFCO and when you attend the Admiralty Interview Board. For the weeks and months leading up to the selection process, be motivated as best you can and always keep your fitness levels up as this will serve to increase your levels of motivation.

Work hard, stay focused and be what you want…

Richard McMunn

P.S. Come and spend a day with my team on the one day intensive Royal Navy Officer AIB preparation course at the following website:

www.NavyOfficerCourse.co.uk

Visit www.how2become.com to find more titles and courses that will help you to pass the Royal Navy Officer selection process, including:

- How to pass the Royal Navy Officer interview.
- 1 Day RN Officer training course.
- Online Royal Navy Officer psychometric testing.
- Psychometric testing books and CD's.

www.how2become.com

Printed in Germany
by Amazon Distribution
GmbH, Leipzig